New Kindle Fire HD Manual

The Complete User Guide to Master Your Kindle Fire HD 8 & 10 (Newbie to Expert)

Vincent McCoy

including specific information will be considered an illegal act irrespective of if it is done electronically or in print. This extends to creating a secondary or tertiary copy of the work or a recorded copy and is only allowed with express written consent from the Publisher. All additional rights reserved.

The information in the following pages is broadly considered to be a truthful and accurate account of facts and as such any inattention, use or misuse of the information in question by the reader will render any resulting actions solely under their purview. There are no scenarios in which the publisher or the original author of this work can be in any fashion deemed liable for any hardship or damages that may befall them after undertaking information described herein.

Additionally, the information in the following pages is intended only for informational purposes and should thus be thought of as universal. As befitting its nature, it is presented without assurance regarding its prolonged validity or interim quality. Trademarks that are mentioned are done without written consent and can in no way be considered an endorsement from the trademark holder.

TABLE OF CONTENTS

INTRODUCTION 1

CHAPTER 1: ALL YOU NEED TO KNOW ABOUT YOUR FIRE HD 3

CHAPTER 2: SHOPPING AND ENTERTAINMENT ON YOUR HD FIRE 41

CHAPTER 3: ALEXA ON THE KINDLE FIRE HD ..77

CHAPTER 4: TROUBLESHOOTING AND COMMON ISSUES WITH YOUR KINDLE FIRE ...97

CONCLUSION 107

CHECK OUT OTHER BOOKS 109

Introduction

Once you have a new technological device it automatically becomes your baby, and you want to ensure that you learn how to set it up properly.

Fortunately for you, I am a *bestselling author* of a number of *How-to Guides* that have helped individuals like you get it right on the first go.

Now, take a deep breath and relax, for you are in good hands. I am going to share information that will assist you in setting up your **Kindle Fire HD 8 or 10**.

I am excited to help you!

Are you excited to learn too?

Great! Let's begin.

Chapter 1: All You Need to Know About Your Fire HD

Charging Your Kindle Fire

It is very likely that your Kindle Fire will require charging from the get-go, so the rule of thumb about charging any new device would also apply to your Kindle Fire HD 8 or 10.

You can utilize one of two methods to get your gadget charged. Either you use the USB cable or the adaptor that came in the box with your Kindle Fire.

If you are using the USB cable, you will have to turn on your computer (that is either fully charged or plugged in as well) then insert the larger end of the USB cable into the USB slot on your computer, and the smaller end of it into your Kindle Fire. The slot for your USB cable is located at the top of your **Kindle Fire HD 8** between the power button and the headphone slot. On the **Kindle Fire HD 10,** it is located on the right side of the device between the power button and the headphone slot.

If you opt to use the adaptor instead, that is not a problem. All you need to do is to insert the smaller end of your adaptor into the charging slot on your Kindle Fire and the other end into an electrical socket.

If you do not see a lightning bolt on your battery icon at the top of your device screen, along with an amber color on the indicator light to the bottom of your Kindle Fire, your device is not being charged. You might need to check to see if your Kindle Fire is properly connected to your power source of choice.

Once your Kindle Fire is fully charged, the indicator light will turn green.

Turning On Your Kindle Fire

Once your device is fully charged, it is time for you to unplug it, turn it on, and start the steps to have your Kindle Fire settings and registration completed. To turn on your Kindle Fire HD 8, look at the top of the device to the left for an icon with the following symbol or for your Kindle Fire HD 10, at the right side of the device. Simply hold down the power button until the device turns on.

First Stages of Settings and Registration

Do not be alarmed if you are unable to access apps and other services the first time you power on your Kindle Fire. Amazon has included a series of steps to help you get started with the set-up process, and this will be evident with the *Welcome Message* which appears on the first screen.

With the guide of this book, after you navigate through all the steps successfully, your Kindle Fire will also be connected to the internet and registered to your Amazon account.

Step 1: Choose the language of your choice for your Kindle Fire with the button that is located on the top left of your **Home Screen**. At the bottom of the screen to the left, you can also choose to enlarge the size of the text on your device if you so desire by using the tab entitled

Text Size. After choosing your device language and text size, click **Continue** at the bottom right of your Kindle Fire.

Step 2: Choose your **Wi-Fi Network** from the list of networks that are provided. You will have to enter your password in the field provided after you have selected it, then click **Connect.** You might have to wait a few seconds for the device to become connected to your Wi-Fi.

Once connected, you might be prompted to update the software. Simply go ahead with the update. After the update is fully installed, your Kindle Fire will restart. This process will take approximately five to seven minutes to complete depending on the speed of your Wi-Fi network.

Step 3: For this stage, ensure you have your Amazon account login information, because you will now be required to register your device on Amazon. Yes, you will need an Amazon account if you want to download all the cool benefits that Amazon offers, including using a Prime or Kindle Unlimited membership.

If you do not have an Amazon account, take a few minutes to create one by selecting the option **New to Amazon? Start Here.**

On the other hand, if you would rather just go and enjoy your Kindle Fire, you can opt to set up the Amazon account at a later date by selecting the option **Complete Setup Later.** If you select **Complete Setup Later**, a pop-up message will appear informing you that you must complete the setup to download books, music, video, apps, and other items on your Kindle Fire. If you decide that you still want to just use your Kindle Fire now, then select **Skip** to proceed to the next step. If you change your mind and you want to complete the registration process, click **Cancel** to return to the set-up page.

For the purposes of this book, I will demonstrate the set-up process.

Back to the registration process: Either you can create an Amazon account to ensure you have the login information, or if you already have an account with Amazon, then you can enter the information now. You will be prompted to ensure that your **Time Zone** is correct. Usually, this will not need any adjustment because it defaults to the time set up on your Wi-Fi. With that said, on the bottom of your screen to the right will be a tab with the word **Continue.**

If you previously owned another Kindle Fire, you will now be able to restore information that was on that Kindle by selecting **Restore Your Fire.** However, for the purposes of this book, I selected **Do Not Restore** to continue to the next step.

Step 4: Relax; I know you are anxious, but you are just a few tabs away from reaching your **Home Screen**. Just a few more options to go before you will be graced with that grand moment.

One of the options that you will now see is **Family Setup.** Here, you can add other adults to your account. Another benefit under the family setup is to *choose to set up a child's profile*. You can have a maximum of four child profiles to download up to 10,000 kid-friendly titles using the Amazon FreeTime Unlimited benefit. Additionally, you can share books, apps, and videos that you purchase with your child. If you do not have a child, no worries! Just select **Not Now** and then tap **Continue** at the bottom right of your screen.

The next benefit is to enable location services if you so desire. While this might be a great benefit to you, it can also be a battery-drainer, so you might want to pass on this benefit unless you really need it. I opted to pass on enabling this benefit by selecting **No Thanks.**

We are now at **Backup & Auto-Save** services; this is a really a good benefit. You want to know that if anything happens to your device, such as it being lost or stolen, your files will be saved on the Amazon Cloud. When you replace your Kindle, should such a misfortune occur, you can always restore your information from Amazon Cloud. Amazon normally has all the backup and auto-save options automatically selected; however, if any of the options are not selected, just ensure you select them before scrolling down to the bottom of your screen to click **Continue**.

Step 5: This is where you will be given the opportunity to **Connect Social Networks.** Isn't it great that you won't have to miss any tweets or feeds from Facebook if you connect your Kindle to your favorite social networks? If you would like to do this, simply follow the prompts to log into your accounts. I left this option for later and scrolled to the bottom of the page to hit **Continue.**

Step 6: Amazon is offering accident coverage. Yes, that's right. This benefit is for protection against accidental damages under a two-year protection plan. So, you can purchase insurance from Amazon to cover your Kindle device. This is another great benefit. But for the purposes of this book, I chose **No thanks, continue without protection.**

Step 7: Here is where Amazon will provide a tutorial about the features of your Kindle Fire. You can choose to look at the tutorial and click **Next** each time to move to the proceeding slide, or you can simply select **Exit** at any time to end the tutorial. Whether you went through all the slides for the tutorial or exited right away, you will finally be able to see your **Home Screen**.

Just as I promised, your device is now connected to Wi-Fi and registered to your Amazon account.

Learning to Navigate and Changing Your Wallpaper

To navigate on your Kindle, you will need to know the function of the following three keys which are located at the bottom of your screen.

The triangle-like button is your **Back** button. You can use this button to go back to a

previous section that you viewed on your
Kindle. For example, if you are browsing the
internet and you click on something that you
did not really want to view, you can use the
Back button to get off that page. The **Back**
button might be used to get to the **Home**
Screen if you click on it enough times.

The circle button is your **Home** button.
You use this to navigate to your **Home Screen**.
No matter what app you are in on your Kindle,
you can click the circle button and you will be
navigated back to your **Home Screen**.

The square button is your **Recent Apps**
button. This is the button that you use to view
all the apps you currently have running or have

recently opened on your Kindle. You can use the **Recent Apps** button to filtrate through the apps that you have running, and go back to one of them if you so desire. It is also an easy way to find out which apps you have running that need to be closed to save on battery usage. To close the apps that are running in the background, press the **Recent Apps** button and use your finger to swipe from right to left to close the apps that you do not need.

Note: *If you open an app or are watching a video, and the navigating buttons are not displayed at the bottom of your screen, you can swipe your finger upwards on the screen and they will be displayed.*

Shortcuts to Navigate

A quicker way of navigating on your Kindle is to go to your **Home Screen**. Look to the top of the screen and you will see a list of tabs such as **Recent**, **Home**, **Books**, **Videos**, **Games**, **Apps**, and so forth. You can also use those to navigate on your Kindle. For example, the Recent tab will take you to the apps that you used recently, and you can easily select which one you would like to use again. The Games tab will take you to your games.

You can swipe back and forth on the screen to switch pages and look for a tab that you might not be seeing.

Note: *If you want to browse the internet, go to your **Home Screen** and look for **Silk Browser.** It will launch to open your internet browser.*

And that's it for the shortcuts to navigate on your tab.

How to Change the Wallpaper on Your Kindle

Go to your **Home Screen** and look for the **Settings** tab, which looks like a small gear. Click on it and select **Display.** Then click **Select Home Screen Wallpaper.** Finally, click **Change Your Home Screen Wallpaper.** You will have the option to choose from **Your Photos** that are stored on your Kindle or to select an image that was pre-installed on your device.

Using the Quick Actions Panel to Change Your Wallpaper

Tap on the **Home Screen** button to navigate to your **Home Screen**. Then use your finger to swipe from the top of your **Home Screen** in a downward motion. You will see the **Quick Actions Panel**. Scroll down and look for the **Settings** tab and click on it. You can then follow the steps previously mentioned to change your wallpaper on your Kindle.

Bluetooth Pairing

With your Kindle Fire HD 8 or 10 Bluetooth paring is available, but certain conditions apply.

Do not get all worked up about the above statement. The conditions that are applied are similar to other Bluetooth pairing devices.

First, you must ensure that whatever you want to pair your Kindle Fire with is compatible with it.

With that said, your Kindle Fire can be paired with most wireless gadgets that have the Bluetooth feature. I am sure you will be happy to know that the following devices can be paired with your Kindle Fire HD 8 or 10:

- **Speakers:** You might want to use Bluetooth speakers to listen your music or watch movies at a higher volume.
- **Keyboards:** You might find it difficult to use the built-in keyboard on your Kindle Fire, so this feature will be beneficial to you when you want to type with a more comfortable gadget.

To pair your device using Bluetooth ensure that the other device is within a pairable distance to your Kindle Fire.

Second, ensure that your accessory for Bluetooth is enabled and in the paring mode. To enable the Bluetooth accessory, use your finger to swipe from the top of your Kindle screen downwards. The **Quick Settings** will be displayed. Select **Wireless** and then **Bluetooth.**

Now, select **On** to enable your **Bluetooth** feature. Once your **Bluetooth** is on, you will see the following icon appear at the top of your Kindle screen to the right side next to the wireless icon.

At this point, your Kindle Fire will start searching for the available pairable devices.

Look for **Available Devices,** and from the list of devices that is displayed, select the gadget that you would like to be paired with your Kindle Fire. A series of pairing instructions will appear; follow them to complete the paring process.

How to Set Up Your Email

Step 1: Navigate to your **Home Screen** or select the **Apps** button at the bottom of your Kindle Fire screen. Search for the **Email** icon among the apps and click on it.

Step 2: From the list of different email providers that appear under the **Add an Account** tab, select the one that you have an account with, and enter your login information. There will be four fields for you to enter information. First you will enter your name, then your email address, your password, and finally you will enter a description. For the description, you can enter the email provider that you are using. This is an easy way to remember which account you have registered on your Kindle Fire. Once all the information is entered into the necessary field, click **Next** located at the bottom right of your screen.

Step 3: You will be given the opportunity to synchronize your contacts and any dates you already have on your Kindle calendar. You can then click **Save** to go to the next step.

Step 4: Select **View Inbox** and you will be navigated to the inbox of your email. If want to read an email just tap on it and it will open.

When you open an email, three tabs will appear to the top right of the Kindle Fire screen. These tabs are: **Delete, Respond,** and **New.**

The **Delete** button, as you might already know, will remove that email from your inbox.

The **Respond** tab will have a drop-down menu with three tabs: **Reply**, **Reply to All**, and **Forward**.

You would select **New** when you want to create a new email. If you click on the plus sign that is located to the top left of the screen when you start a new email, it will provide you with a list of your email contacts to send an message to.

Note: *A really great feature of the Kindle Fire when you are in your email inbox is that if you turn the device sideways, the screen will rotate and divide the contents of your inbox into sections. With the new interface, to the left of the Kindle Fire screen you will be able to view the other emails that are in your inbox. To the right, the email that you had opened will be displayed.*

*To the left of the screen at the top, you will see the tab called **Main Page.** If you click on **Show Folders,** you will be able to see all of your other folders such as your **Spam Box**, **Starred**, **Deleted** and so forth.*

If you want to add a second email account while you are in your inbox, select **Menu** next to the **New** tab. From the **Menu** tab you will see the option to **Add Account,** and you can follow the previous steps mentioned to add an email account.

How to Receive Email Notifications on Your Kindle Fire

Even though you have already added your email account to your Kindle Fire, you will not automatically receive notifications on your Kindle Fire for new emails. That is why I am about to demonstrate the necessary steps to set up the notification feature for emails on your Kindle Fire.

Step 1: Swipe from the top of your Kindle Fire screen in a downward motion and select **More.** Then tap **Settings.**

Step 2: Scroll down and click **Applications.** Under **Applications** you see **Notifications Settings.** Select that option.

Step 3: Under **Notification Settings** you will find a tab called **Email.** Click on it. Then, select **On** which is located to the right of the **Email** tab.

Note: *When you set up your email, the notification tab is automatically turned off, which is why you will not receive notifications about new emails unless you follow the above steps to turn on the notifications.*

How to Set Up a Timer for Emails

Now that you have your email address(es) added to your Kindle Fire and have taken care of getting the notifications at the top of the device screen, it is time for me to show you how often your Kindle Fire should submit the notifications about new emails. If you are someone that uses your email a lot to communicate with business associates or loved ones, then you will find this section very useful.

Step 1: Follow previous steps to access your **Settings,** then **Applications,** and scroll down to the option **Email, Contacts, and Calendar.**

Step 2: Scroll down to select the email account that you would like to receive frequent notifications for on your Kindle Fire.

Step 3: Scroll down to **Inbox Check Frequency.** Then set the timer for how often you want to be notified about new emails.

Note: *If you want to receive the emails as soon as they enter your inbox, then you need to select the tab **Automatic (push).***

How to Download Apps and Games on Your Kindle Fire

Step 1: Navigate to your **Apps** screen by either using the **Apps** button at the bottom of your screen, or by using the shortcut at the top of your **Home Screen**.

Step 2: Once you navigate to the **Apps** screen, select **Shop** located to the top right corner of your screen.

Step 3: Select the **Search** icon at the top right corner of your screen and type in the name of the app or game that you would like to download. Once the app or game appears, click on it and look for the **Download** button.

In those three simple steps you can download any app or game available in the shop.

How to Download Videos on Your Kindle Fire

Step 1: Navigate to your home page and use the shortcut at the top of your screen to locate the **Videos** tab.

Step 2: At the top right corner of your screen, you will see the **Shop** tab. Click on it.

Step 3: Select the **Search** icon at the top right corner of your screen, and then type in the name of the video you would like to download. When the video you searched for appears, you can click on it and look for the download button.

How to Uninstall an App from Your Kindle Fire

First, let me inform you that not all apps on your Kindle Fire can be deleted. There are some pre-installed apps that come with your Kindle Fire that you will not be able to remove from the device. These include **Calendar**, **Contacts**, and **Email** just to name a few.

However, any apps or games that you download onto your Kindle Fire yourself can be uninstalled.

Below is the first and easiest way to uninstall an app.

Step 1: Navigate to the **Home Screen** using either the **Home Screen** button, or use the **Apps** button to go to apps.

Step 2: Locate the app that you would like to uninstall from your device. Once you have found the app, use your finger to press down on it for a few seconds. Two options will appear. The first option is **Add to Favorites,** and the second option is **Delete.** Select **Delete**, and in a few seconds the app will be deleted from your Kindle Fire screen.

How to Deal with Pop-Up Messages When You Are Uninstalling an App

Not all apps will be deleted immediately when you select the **Delete** tab. Here's what to do when you experience a pop-up message when you are deleting an app.

Step 1: Follow the previous steps to navigate to the app that you would like to uninstall.

Step 2: Once you have located the app, use your finger to press down on the app, then select **Delete**. A pop-up message will appear asking if you are sure you want to delete this app. Click **OK** at the bottom right of your Kindle Fire screen. You will be navigated to a second screen that also says **OK.** Click on that tab and your device will uninstall the app.

How to Uninstall a Game from Your Kindle Fire

Uninstalling a game from your Kindle Fire is done in a similar way to how you would delete an app.

Step 1: Navigate to the **Home Screen** using the **Home Screen** button. Then select **Games** at the top of your Kindle Fire screen.

Step 2: Locate the game that you would like to uninstall from your device. Once you have found the game, use your finger to press down on it for a few seconds. Two options will appear. First option is **Add to Favorites** and the second option is **Delete.** Select **Delete,** and in a few seconds the game will be deleted from your Kindle Fire screen.

Features for Everyone in the Family

You can change the color of the built-in keyboard on your Kindle Fire by swiping your finger downwards from the top of your screen to go to your **Quick Panel.** Then select **Settings.**

Look to the right for the **Keyboard and Language** option and click on it.

Select **Fire Keyboard** on the bottom left of the list of options.

Now select the first tab, **Keyboard Color**, and a pop-up will appear with two options. The options are either **Dark** or **Light,** so you can choose your preferred color.

Note: *The dark option will give you a black keyboard and the light option will give you a white keyboard.*

Adding Secondary Keys to Your Keyboard

You can add more characters to the built-in keyboard on your Kindle Fire by swiping your finger from the top of your device screen to go to your **Quick Panel.** Then select **Settings.** Look to the right for the **Keyboard and Language** option and click on it.

Select **Fire Keyboard** on the bottom left of the list of options. Look for the tab which reads **Secondary Keys** and click on it.

Now select the first option, **Secondary Keys on All Rows.**

Note: *All the special characters such as the $ sign will appear on the keyboard, which will make typing much easier.*

Installing Honeypot on Your Kindle Fire

I know that I do not need to write a lot about the dangers of viruses and hackers that are lurking around on the internet trying to find a device that is unprotected to invade.

One of the best virus protection software that is creating a big buzz in the technological world is called **Honeypot**.

To help protect your Kindle Fire from viruses and hackers, you might want to think about installing **Honeypot** software on your device.

It is always better to be safe sorry. So, protect your device for a better chance of stopping any unwanted invasion of your Kindle Fire.

How to Have a Multi-Screen So You Can Multi-Task

First, download the **Multi-Screen Multi-Tasking App** – this is a *free* app by the way, so no worries about not having money to purchase it.

After you have downloaded the **Multi-Screen Multi-Tasking App**, go to your apps screen, search for the feature, and click on it.

This app allows you to work with multiple screens at a time. For example, if you should select the **Globe** icon at the bottom to the left of the screen, which will allow you to open a web browser. You can use your finger to move the browser to one section of the screen. Then, you can click on the **Globe** icon a second time to open another browser. With two web browsers now open on the app, you can research two topics at the same time!

This app will be extra useful when conducting research because there is a **Note Pad** located on the menu bar of the app. This will make it very easy to jot down points as you read articles.

If you enjoy listening to music while you work, a music icon is also located on the menu bar of the app.

Chapter 2: Shopping and Entertainment on Your HD Fire

When speaking about a Kindle Fire, the first thing that comes to most people's mind is shopping or downloading books. So, this book would not be complete without a section about shopping and entertainment on your Kindle Fire.

How to Buy and Read Books, Magazines, and Periodicals

Step 1: Use the **Home Screen** button to navigate to your Kindle Fire **Home Screen**.

From the list of tabs at the top of the screen, select **Books**.

Step 2: You will see two tabs: one labeled **Cloud** and one labeled **Device**.

The **Cloud** tab is for books that you have stored on **Amazon Cloud**, and **Device** is for any books that you will now download directly onto your Kindle Fire.

Note: *The books in your **Cloud** can be downloaded at any time to your Kindle Fire by selecting the **Download** arrow located at the bottom of each book.*

Now, let's get back to shopping for books!

On the top left of your screen, you will see the **Shopping** icon. Tap on it, type in the name of the book you would like to purchase, and click **Search**.

Step 3: When you locate the book that you would like to purchase, tap on it. You will be given the option to either download the entire book, or a trial sample. I would recommend trying the trial sample wherein you will be able to download a few pages of the book to read before you make a purchase.

When you choose to download a trial sample, you will see a tab with the words **Read Sample Now.** Select it, and you will be able to read the sample pages immediately.

If you like the sample pages that are downloaded to your Kindle Fire, you can tap on the **Back** button which will take you back to the purchasing page. There, you can purchase the book and have the entire book downloaded to your Kindle Fire.

However, if you do not like the book, you can still use the **Back** button to return to the previous page and cancel the order.

How to Download Free Books to Your Kindle Fire

Step 1: Follow the previous steps to access your book app. Once the book app is located, type **Free Books** into the **Search** box, and all the free books on Amazon will be listed.

Step 2: When you see a title you like, tap on it to select it and download it. If you do not see a download tab, and you see a tab with the word **Buy,** then click on it. You will still receive the book free of charge.

Note: *You can also filter your search by searching for books in a specific genre that you love to read. All you have to do is type the word "free" before the genre of your choice.*

How to Remove a Book from Your Kindle Fire

It is important to know how to remove a book from your Kindle Fire to free up more storage space on your device. Plus, it makes no sense keeping a title that you have already read and have no intention of reading again.

Note: *You cannot delete the Oxford Dictionary that came with your Kindle Device. You will only be allowed to delete books that you directly downloaded to your Kindle Fire.*

Step 1: Navigate to your **Home Screen** and look for the **Books** tab at the top of your screen. It should be among the first set of tabs. If you do not see it, just swipe your finger on the list of tabs from right to left to view the other buttons.

Step 2: When you enter the **Books** app, ensure that the tab **Device** is *orange.* If not, you will be deleting books from your Amazon Cloud and not from the Kindle Fire itself.

Step 3: Search for the book you would like to delete by scrolling through the list of books on your device. After you locate the book, press down on it until you see the tabs **Add to Favorite** and **Delete**. Click **Delete,** and in a few seconds, the book will be removed from your device.

Happy reading! It is now time to learn how to get your favorite beats.

How to Transfer Files to Your Kindle Fire

The **USB Cable** that came with your Kindle Fire will be very handy in performing this process. If for some reason you did not receive one, then you will have to purchase a USB cable to transfer files to your Kindle Fire.

Step 1: Connect the smaller end of your **USB cable** to your Kindle Fire – you will find the slot at the top of the device for Kindle Fire 8 and at the side for Kindle Fire 10.

Insert the larger end of the USB cable into your computer.

Step 2: Ensure that your Kindle Fire is turned on by swiping your finger across the screen to unlock the device. If it needs to be powered up, press the power button to turn it on.

Step 3: A message will appear on your Kindle Fire screen informing you that you can transfer files from your computer.

On your computer, a pop-up box will appear on the screen once it has identified your Kindle Fire. Select **Open Folder to View Files** by double-clicking on it.

Note: *If the pop-up box does not appear on your computer screen, click on **Start – My Computer – Kindle Fire**. Then double-click the Kindle tab, and it will open your device folders.*

Step 4: Say, for example, you want to transfer a PDF file to from your computer to your Kindle Fire: click on the file and hold down on the cursor to drag it to the Kindle Fire document folder, then release your finger from the cursor. You will see a pop-up message informing you that the file is being copied to your Kindle Fire.

Another method to transfer a file from your computer to your Kindle Fire is to follow the previous steps connecting your USB cable to your devices. Then right-click on the file you want to transfer and select either **Copy** or **Cut**.

Then open the Kindle Fire folder you want to transfer the file into, right click anywhere in the folder, and select **Paste**.

Note*: You can use these transfer methods to move any documents, videos, photos, and music from your computer to and from your Kindle Fire.*

How to Download YouTube on Your Kindle Fire

Most individuals will go to YouTube to view music videos, so I am going to show you how to get the official YouTube feature on your Kindle Fire.

Step 1: You will need to download an app by the name of **1Mobile Market** – this is a free app. *This feature allows you to have access to a* *lot of the apps that you will not see in the Amazon App store or the Android App store.*

Swipe from the top of your Kindle Fire screen downwards to access the **Quick Panel** and then click **Settings.** In **Settings,** select **Applications** and turn on **Apps from Unknown Sources.** Click **OK** on the pop-up message that will appear. Then use the **Home Screen** button to navigate to your Kindle **Home Screen**.

Step 2: Click **Web** on your **Home Screen** at the top and type in the words **1Mobile Market,** then click **Search**.

Step 3: When the **1Mobile Market** page loads, scroll down and look to the right for **Scan to Download** and tap that option.

Step 4: Look to the right for **Download** and click on it. A pop-up message will appear asking you, **Download File?** Click on **OK** and the file will start downloading. In a few seconds, the download should be completed depending on your Wi-Fi network speed.

Step 5: You will need to download a file manager. Go to **Apps** on your **Home Screen**. Then click **Store** which is located on the top right corner of the screen. In the **Search** box, type the words **File Manager Free** and click **Search**. Normally, it is the second option that will appear: **File Manager Free.** Click on the app and tap **Download**. After it finishes downloading, click **Open**.

Step 6: Scroll down and select the folder **Downloads**. You will see the **1Mobile Market**

file that you previously downloaded; click on it. You will be asked, **Do you want to install this application?** Click **Next** at the bottom right of the page. Then select **Install** at the bottom right of the page.

Finally, tap **Done** and select the **Home Screen** icon at the bottom to the right of your screen.

Note: *When you are searching for the* ***1Mobile Market*** *app, ensure that your app setting is on* ***Device*** *and not* ***Cloud.***

Step 7: Click on the ***1Mobile Market*** app and, in the search bar, type **YouTube** and tap **Search**. Scroll down and look for the *official YouTube app*. Once you located official **YouTube** app, click on it and select **Download** which is located to the left of the screen.

Step 8: Use your finger to swipe the top of your screen in a downward motion and, once the YouTube app download is completed, tap on it. Now look to the bottom right of your screen and select **Install**.

Step 9: When the installation is completed, click **Open** and it will take you to **YouTube**.

Note: One downside to this is that you will not be able to log in to your personal YouTube channel because Kindle Fire is an Amazon device and is technically incompatible. You can, however, continue as a guest.

How to Download YouTube Videos on Your Kindle Fire

Step 1: Go to your home page and tap on the **Web** button. Then type the phrase "tubemate.net" in the search bar and click on the **Search** icon.

Step 2: Select the option that says **Download Handster**.

Step 3: Press the **Download** button on the left below the word "free." *If you click on the **Download** button and a pop-up message does not appear, press and hold the **Download** button for a few seconds.*

When the pop-up message appears, click **Open**. The app will then start to download. After it finishes downloading, click **Install** located at the bottom right of your screen.

Let me just stop here and address a question that you might be asking. Why do you need this app? Well, this app is not in your Amazon App store because if you have access to YouTube videos, then you are less likely to spend money on Amazon Videos. So, you must have this app to make YouTube work on the Amazon platform.

Step 4: Now tap **Open** at the bottom right of your screen. A pop-up message will appear telling you how to use the app, and you can download **YouTube** videos using the green **Download** button.

Now, go to **YouTube,** type in the name of a video, and click the **Search** button. When you see the video, you can select and start watching it. If you look to the bottom right of the screen, you will see a very large green **Download** button. Click on it. A pop-up message will appear; click the box that says **Do not show me this message again**.

Drum roll moment!

The next pop-up message will ask you if you want to **Download the Video** or **Continue Watching.**

Click **Download**.

Another cool feature that comes with the **tubemate.net** is that if you look at the bottom of your YouTube video screen where the green **Download** button is, you will also see a **Folder** tab. Open the **Folder** and you will find videos that were downloaded to your Kindle Fire successfully. You can choose to change the format of the videos you downloaded by tapping on any one of them. A pop-up message will appear with various options. Among those options are: **Play as Video, Play as Music, Go to YouTube, Convert to MP3, Save as MP3, Delete File, and Remove from List.**

This is a multi-tasking app that is *free* and can save you time if you want to convert your video files. Additionally, when you have no internet connection, you can go to **Apps – Tubemate – Downloads** and click on any of the videos that you downloaded to your device. A pop-up message will appear with two options: **Start over** or **Resume Playing**.

You will now have few more dollars in your pocket since you will not have to purchase a lot of videos from Amazon.

Note: *Before you move onto our next feature, go back into* *Settings – Applications* *and turn off* *Apps from Unknown Sources.* *If you do not turn off* *Apps from Unknown Sources,* *you leave your device open for viruses to be downloaded onto it.*

How to Download Music onto Your Kindle Fire

Step 1: Go to your **Music** app and select the **Store** tab that is located at the top right of your Kindle Fire screen.

Note: *The* *Cloud* *tab will display all the music that you have ever purchased from Amazon,* *and the **Device** tab will show all of the music that you actually downloaded onto your Kindle Fire.*

Step 2: In the **Kindle Music Store,** music is divided into different categories. You might see the **Album Deals** in the first category on the page. Next, you might see **New Releases** or **Recommendations from Amazon** based on your past purchases. You can just continue scrolling to view the different categories that are listed in the music store.

When you have finished looking through the different categories and are ready to make a purchase, you will need to search for the song or album that you want to buy.

Step 2: Type either the name of the artist, album, or song into the search bar and click the icon to search.

When you find the artist/album/song, you will need to double-click on it **Price** tab to initiate the buying process.

If you just want one song from the album, tap on the name of the album to view the songs that are on it. When the list of the songs is displayed, you will need to look through the list for the one that you would like to buy and click on **Price** located to the right of the song.

The **Price** tab color will change to **green,** and the word **Buy** will appear on it. Click on the green **Buy** tab to move to next step of purchasing the song.

What is really awesome about using this feature is that if you are viewing the list of songs on the album and you happen to see a song that you had no idea that artist had released, you can listen to a 30-second clip of the song for *free*. To listen the free 30 seconds of any of the songs, just press the **Play** button located to the left of each song.

Step 3: A pop-up message will appear informing you that your purchase is completed, and that the song is saved in your **Amazon Cloud Player**.

You will also be given the three options. You can now go to your music library to play or download the song, return to your Kindle Fire, or continue shopping.

Select **Go to Library**.

Step 4: A pop-up message will appear asking you if you would like to automatically download your song and all future MP3 purchases that you make to your Kindle Fire.

First, select the box beside the statement that says *Don't ask me again,* and then click **Yes.**

Note: *This last step will ensure that in the future, that pop-up message will not appear, and your purchases will automatically be downloaded to your Kindle Fire.*

Step 5: Your song is now being downloaded to your Kindle Fire. After the download is complete, you may find your song in your music app under the tab **Device**.

Note: If you have a song stored in your Amazon Cloud that you would like to download to your Kindle Fire, you can go to your **Music** app by selecting the **Cloud** tab at the top of your screen, looking for the song, and pressing down on it until a pop-up menu appears with the following options:

- Add to Play List
- Shop this Artist
- Download Song

Select **Download Song** from the list of options and it will automatically download the song.

I hope you will enjoy rocking to your beats on your Kindle Fire.

How to Download Audiobooks onto Your Kindle Fire

Step 1: There is an app that is built-in on your Kindle Fire called **Audible.com** that you will need to search for in your **Kindle Fire Apps.** The Audible.com app comes with a free 30-day subscription trial, and you will also be given one *free credit that can purchase an audiobook*.

You will also be given a **30%** discount on any audiobooks that you purchase with the exception of the one that you will be using your *free credit* to purchase.

Note: *There is no harm in trying this benefit for the 30-day free trial, and if you cannot afford* *the subscription fee, then you can choose to cancel your membership before the 30-day free trial expires.*

Step 2: Locate and click on the Audible.com app. Select **I Am New to Audible**.

Step 3: Select your **Country**.

Step 4: The Audible.com app has a few audiobooks that were pre-installed on it. If you have never listened to an audiobook, you can select one these free audiobooks to get a feel for what an audiobook is like. You can view the cover of books, the summary, and the chapter headings from Audible.com using the menu bar at the top of the screen.

If you just want to purchase your own audiobooks, then press the **Back** button. Now, look for **Shopping Cart** on the top left of your screen and tap on it.

Step 5: Type in the name of the audiobook that you would like to purchase in the search bar and then click **Search**.

Step 6: Click on the book and select **Buy**. You will be prompted to log in to your Amazon account; do so and then select your payment method.

Step 7: To access the audiobook that you purchased, log in to Audible.com. The login information for Audible.com will automatically become the same information used to login to your Amazon account. After you are logged in,

Audible.com will activate your Kindle Fire, and the book will commence downloading to your device.

Step 8: Click on the **Update** button that is located to the top left of your Kindle Fire screen. Once you tap on the **Update** button, you will see the audiobook that you purchased in your library.

Step 9: Click the **Download** arrow located to the left of the audiobook. After the audiobook finishes downloading, tap on it for the audio to begin.

You can use the buttons at the bottom of the screen to **Pause**, **Play**, and **Stop** the audio. You can use the menu at the top of the screen to see the chapters if you desire.

Have a great listen! Or continue reading my book to find out about another cool another feature.

How to Use a Bluetooth Speaker with Your Kindle Fire

Step 1: Use your finger to swipe from the top of your Kindle Fire screen downwards, and select the **More** tab located at the top right corner of your device.

Step 2: Click on **Wireless** and then **Bluetooth**. You will have to turn on the **Bluetooth;** click the button with the **On/Off** options, and ensure that **On** is *orange.* Next, click **Search** at the bottom of your screen.

Step 3: Turn on the **Bluetooth** feature of your speaker and put it into pairing mode. When you see the **Bluetooth light** flashing on your speaker, that means the pairing mode has been enabled.

Step 4: Now, you will need to tap on the button at the bottom of your Kindle Fire screen that says **Search for Device**.

Step 5: Once your Kindle Fire locates the speaker, the name of it will appear on the screen. Click on the name of the speaker and it will begin the pairing process.

When the pairing is completed, you will see the word **Connected** appear below the name of the speaker on your Kindle Screen.

You can go ahead now and test the volume of Kindle Fire using the speaker.

How to Mirror Your Kindle Fire Screen to Your TV

Important: *For this feature to work you MUST have a smart TV. If you have a regular tube TV, this feature will NOT be able to work with it. Your TV MUST have an HMI free input that you can plug it into; without the HMI input, this feature will NOT work.*

*Before you attempt to add this feature, you must also purchase a cable that has an **HMI** connection on the large end and a **Micro-HDMI** connection on the smaller end.*

Step 1: Insert the larger end of the USB cable into your television set and the smaller end into your Kindle Fire.

Step 2: Now, pull back a little from the television. You will notice that everything that is on your Kindle Fire screen is also on your TV screen. If you swipe your finger across your Kindle Fire, you will see that same movement is happening on your TV screen.

You can browse on the internet using your Kindle Fire and it will show on your television. If you want to watch a movie or YouTube video, it will also show on your television screen. You can open your books or even check your social media accounts, and it will be shown on your television screen as long as your Kindle Fire remains connected to the TV. Essentially, anything you do on your Kindle Fire while it is connected to your television will also be shown on your TV screen.

Well, that's it for connecting your Kindle Fire to the big screen. Let us move on to more features.

How to Take Pictures with the Camera on Your Kindle Fire

Step 1: Swipe all the way to the left on your Kindle Fire screen until you see the tab **Photos**; click on it.

Step 2: Tap on the **Camera** icon that is located at the top right of your Kindle Fire screen.

Step 3: You now have access to your camera. Wave your hand in front of your Kindle Fire, and you will see it on the camera. Tap on the

Camera button that is located to the left of the screen and you will be able to snap a picture.

Note: The resolution of the Kindle Fire camera is not very high, so the quality of your pictures might not be great.

Step 4: You can tap on the pictures on the bottom of your screen to view them and swipe to see the others in your picture queue.

One really great feature that is associated with your camera is that if you look to the right side of the screen, you will see a tab for you to **Email** the pictures from the camera app.

If you want to delete a photo, the **Delete** tab is also located on the right side of your **Camera** app screen.

To **Share** the pictures, there is a folder above the **Delete** tab located to the right of the **Camera** app. Click it to see the icon to share your pictures.

Step 5: Below the **Email** tab, you will see an arrow. Use that arrow to go back, and it will navigate you to your **Picture Folder**. Inside your **Picture Folder**, you will see all the pictures you have taken with your camera. You will also find pictures that you have shared, and those that you uploaded onto your Kindle Fire.

Now you can snap, snap away and store your treasured moments using your Kindle Fire camera app.

Chapter 3: Alexa on the Kindle Fire HD

A lot of buzz has been generating about Alexa among those who are crazy about technological gadgets.

Do you know what Alexa is?

Amazon has decided to make a big step up with its Kindle Fire HD 8 & 10 by ensuring that it has an Alexa among the features of this gadget.

With Alexa, your finger can take a break from all the tapping it used to have to do on your

Kindle Fire, and instead you can simply speak to navigate to different features.

In case you still don't quite understand what Alexa is all about, let me give you the low-down on what exactly Alexa can do.

Think of Alexa as a personal technological assistance software which is voice activated. The Alexa App is available in the Amazon App store, and was created as a companion for the Alexa-enabled Kindle Fire tablets.

The Amazon Kindle Fire HD 10 is a first-of-its-kind tablet to be equipped with the all the features of the Amazon Echo. This is also inclusive of hands-free mode or a voice activator.

Once you enable the Alexa software on your Kindle Fire 10, you can ask questions about the weather, news, or sports, or even give it voice commands to play music, search the internet, or navigate to various apps and features on your Kindle Fire 10.

Take for example if your tablet is on your bed or desk and the screen is locked. You can say out loud: "Alexa, what is the weather like in Japan?" and it will automatically light up with a weather report being displayed on your Kindle Fire screen for the entire week. And this is the best part: *you will hear Alexa responding to your question with the correct answer.*

You can ask Alexa a variety of questions. For example: How old is the Earth? When did the iPhone 10 come out? Who is the president of

France? You can even give it commands, such as: Set an alarm for a specific time or Open audible on my Kindle.

Will you get a correct response? You can bet your bottom dollar you will!

If you find that unbelievable, then just ask Alexa what your location is. *Oh wait, we haven't learned how to enable Alexa on your Kindle Fire! Before reading the steps to enable Alexa, take a minute to read the important notice in the next paragraph.*

Important: *Alexa is NOT available on any of the older generations Kindle Fire tablets. If you decide to download the Alexa App to try this feature, and your device does NOT have the Alexa-enabled feature, the app will NOT work* *on your Kindle Fire. Based on the country you reside in, some of the Alexa features might not be available.*

How to Enable Alexa on Your Kindle Fire

You are not going to believe how incredibly easy it is to activate the Alexa on your Kindle Fire HD.

Get ready to be amazed!

Step 1: Ensure your Kindle Fire is turned on, then navigate to the **Home Screen**. Now, press down on the Kindle Fire **Home** icon until a *blue line* appears.

The *blue line* is your indicator to inform you that Alexa is ready to work for you.

What are you waiting for? Didn't I tell you it would be incredibly easy to activate Alexa? Go ahead now and give it a command.

Some Dos and Don'ts with Alexa

I know that it sounds super-cool to say, "**Alexa,**" but guess what? You **do not** have to call the gadget's name each time you give it a command.

If you are like me and tend to get annoyed very easily when things block your vision on your Kindle Fire, then you might want to remove the Alexa visual if it appears on your screen. To remove the Alexa visual, click on the **Back** button at the bottom of your Kindle Fire screen.

If you turn on the Alexa, obviously you will need to know how to turn it off too, right?

To turn Alexa off, swipe the top of Kindle Fire screen downwards. Select **Settings – Device Options**, then click on the Alexa icon.

Note: *You can also use the previous steps to turn on the Alexa when you are ready. If you have a 7th generation Kindle Fire HD 10, then the steps to turn off Alexa are a little different. You would go to **Settings**, then click on the Alexa icon to turn it off or on.*

Alexa is **not** enabled by default on **Children's Edition** Kindles or if there is a device that has a **Parental Control** *feature.*

If your Kindle Fire has a *child or secondary adult profile,* Alexa will *not* work on that device.

Alexa's hands-free mode *cannot work* with Kindles that do *not* have the 5.5.0.0 or later software.

Using Alexa to Perform Different Functions on Your Kindle Fire

Activating Hands-Free Mode

Navigate to your **Home Screen**, then use your finger to swipe from the top of your Kindle Fire screen downwards. Select **Settings – Alexa – Hands-Free Mode.**

To control your Kindle ESP (Echo Spatial Perception) behavior so that it doesn't respond every time it comes into contact with another

Echo gadget, access **Settings** by navigating to your **Home Screen** and swiping from the top of your Kindle Fire in a downwards motion. Click on the **Alexa** icon and click on the tab **Tablet ESP Behavior.**

Note: *Alexa normally acts up in this way when there is more than one device that is equipped with the Alexa feature that uses a similar wake word.*

Using Alexa to Listen to Various Audio Features on Your Kindle Fire

If you are an audio learner or listener, Alexa can make your life a little easier when you use different audio commands.

When you are feeling the beat of the music in your heart and want to rock your feet to some of your favorite songs, use the following **Alexa voice commands** to get your music playing on your Kindle Fire:

- Play

- Play some music

- Play (state the name of the song)

- Play some (be specific about the genre you would like to listen)

- Resume

Change the Volume of Your Music

Give Alexa the following commands:

- Volume up

- Volume down

- Set volume to level (state the level or number)

Ask Alexa About a Song Title or Artist Name

Did you just hear a song you like, but don't know the name of the song or artist?

Ask Alexa the following questions:

-What is this?

-Who is this?

-What song is this?

-Who is this artist?

-When did this song/album come out?

Okay, so you like that song and want to hear it again. Tell Alexa to play the song again with the following command:

- Repeat this song

Here are some other commands that can be used for Alexa when you are playing music:

- Loop

- Shuffle

- Stop Shuffle

- Next

- Previous

- Skip

- Show me my playlist

- Show me (state a specific genre) list (this is for Echo gadgets with a screen)

- Play me some songs I have not listened to in a while

- Thumbs up (when you like a song when using Pandora, Amazon music, and iHeartRadio)

- Thumbs down (when you do not like a song when using Pandora, Amazon music, and iHeartRadio)

- Play songs from (state the specific city)

How to Stop Music to Answer a Phone Call

I think I just heard your telephone ringing, so why not pause or stop the music with these commands:

- Stop

- Pause

Using Alexa for Audiobooks on Your Kindle Fire

Important: When using the Alexa feature for a book, it will NOT show the text of the book on *the screen, or even activate the immersion reading on your device.*

The audio controls will still be visible at the bottom of your Kindle Fire screen even though you are using Alexa. If you choose to dismiss the visual, the audio will continue to play on your device.

If you would like to use the visual after you dismissed it, you can swipe from the top of your Kindle Fire screen in a downwards motion and you will be able to see the player controls.

To get Alexa to select a title you would like to listen to, give it the following commands:

- Read (state the book title)
- Play the book (state the book title)

- Play the audiobook (state the book title)
- Play (state the book title) from Audible

You can tell Alexa when to pause the book with the following commands:

- Set a sleep timer for (state the specific time in minutes or hours)
- Stop reading the book in (state the specific time in minutes or hours)
- Cancel sleep timer

If you do not remember much about the chapter that you were reading, Alexa can help you with this command:

- Restart

Oh, wait you think it might be another chapter you reached? You can tell Alexa which chapter you think you want to read now with this command:

- Go to chapter (state the chapter number)

Here are some other commands that you might use with Alexa for audiobooks:

- Go back
- Go forward
- Next chapter
- Previous chapter
- Resume my book
- Pause

Alexa Commands for Books that Are Not Audiobooks

Important: To locate books that are eligible to be used with the Alexa feature go to **Alexa– Menu – Music, Videos & Books.** Click **Books.** Under this category you will see the **Kindle** option. You must select your type of device from the drop-down menu before you can select a title to read.

Some Book Reading Commands for Alexa:

- Play the Kindle book (state the specific name of the title)
- Pause
- Stop
- Resume

Books that Can Be Used with the Alexa Feature Are as Follows:

- Books that you purchased from the Kindle Store
- Books that you borrowed from Kindle Owners' Lending Library
- Books that you borrowed from Kindle Unlimited or Prime Reading
- Books that were shared with you in your Family Library

Books that Cannot Be Used with the Alexa Feature Are as Follows:

- Comics
- Graphic novels
- Narration that uses speed control
- Immersion reading

Alexa can be used with many different things on your Kindle Fire, including searching the web and shopping for you. To activate the voice purchasing feature, you will need to go to your **Alexa** app look to the left of the screen for the **Menu** icon. Tap on **Settings** and click on the tab with the words **Voice Purchasing**.

Using Alexa to purchase items for you will only work if you have a *United States billing address and have enabled the one-click payment method on your Amazon account.*

All the best using your Alexa feature, and if you are using it to read this book, you can now say; "Alexa, go to the next chapter."

Chapter 4: Troubleshooting and Common Issues with Your Kindle Fire

Every gadget comes with its own issues, and the Kindle Fire is no exception. Below are some common issues that you might encounter, and solutions to those issues.

Kindle Fire Cannot Connect to Wi-Fi

While there are many different reasons that this problem might exist, one of the main problems is that your Kindle Fire could be in **Airplane Mode**.

Amazon recently changed its device settings for turning off Wi-Fi and 3G connection. To turn off your Wi-Fi connection on your Kindle Fire, you have to use the **Airplane Mode.**

If you see an icon that looks like a plane on your Kindle Fire screen next to the **Battery Charging** indicator, then your device is in **Airplane Mode**.

To disable **Airplane Mode**, go to **Menu** (using the **Quick Panel** steps that were previously mentioned) – **Settings –Airplane Mode**. Look to the right of the **Airplane Mode** tab and you will see the **On/Off** button. Click on it to turn off the **Airplane Mode** on your Kindle Fire.

If the Airplane Mode is not the cause of your Wi-Fi issues, then try the following methods:

- Restart your Kindle Fire.

- Download and install the free **Wi-Fi Analyze** app, which can assist in detecting if the strength of your Wi-Fi is the cause of the issue.

- Check if your router is set for the wrong channel; it might be unsupported.

Kindle Fire Screen Flickering

This issue is one that tests one's patience and anger level, but it might be solved with the simple step of adjusting the brightness of your Kindle Fire. Access the **Notifications** tab at the top of the screen by using your finger to swipe downwards from the top of your screen, then click on **Brightness** and tap **Off** for the **Auto-Brightness** button.

If that does not work, you might want to check or remove the cover that you placed on your Kindle Fire to see if it might be the cause of the problem.

You could also try contacting Amazon through the **Mayday** feature and request a replacement Kindle Fire.

The Crashing or The Freezing of Your Silk Browser

If you enabled any P**arental Control** features on your Kindle Fire, this might be the cause of this problem because it blocks access by default. Access your **Settings** tab, then, go to **Parental Controls** to turn off the feature.

Clearing your **Silk Browser Data** might also assist to resolve this issue. You can clear the

Silk Browser Data by accessing **Settings –
Applications – Manage All Applications – Silk
Browser – Clear Data.**

Kindle Fire Not Charging

A very keynote when looking at charging issues
is: What are you using to charge your Kindle
Fire?

Now, if you are using your USB cable and
attaching it to your computer, your Kindle Fire
can take approximately 13 hours to be fully
charged.

However, if you should use the optional
charger or the cable Amazon issued with your
Kindle Fire, it should take approximately 4
hours to be fully charged.

With that said, ensure that you are using the charging gadgets that came with your Kindle Fire before you contact Amazon about charging issues.

If that is not the cause of the issue, check if your charger is plugged into the electrical socket properly.

Power down your Kindle Fire and try charging it while it is turned off.

You can also check to see if your Kindle Fire has any loose ports. If it does, you can contact Amazon for a replacement.

MicroSD Card Is Not Recognized or Does Not Work

This is a common problem for Kindle Fire users, so if you find that you too have this issue, try the following solutions.

Ensure that your Kindle Fire is fully charged; then press and hold the power button for approximately 40 seconds for the device to force reset itself.

You could also connect to your Wi-Fi network and leave your Kindle Fire for a few minutes to allow it to automatically download and install any updates that are available on your device.

Still having the problem? Remove the MicroSD card from your Kindle Fire for a few minutes, then carefully replace the MicroSD card and try using it.

Ensure the case on your Kindle Fire – if you have one – is not pressing down on the MicroSD card.

Erratic Keyboard Typing

If your Kindle Fire is randomly typing a collection of characters other than what you are trying to type, deleting words, or skipping pages by itself, try some of the following solutions.

Clean your Kindle Fire screen with a *microfiber piece of cloth*.

If your Kindle Fire is in a case, ensure it is correctly fitted.

Power down your Kindle Fire for a while by holding down on the power button for approximately 20 seconds.

Trying a **Factory Reset** is very risky, and you will lose all your content. Therefore, only do this if you have no other choice, and ensure you backup your content first.

To do the **Factory Reset,** you will need to navigate to your **Home Screen** and use your finger to swipe from the top of your screen in a downward motion. Click on **Settings – Device – Reset to Factory Default – Reset.**

If you conduct a factory reset and the issue still exists, then the only option left is to contact Amazon.

Issues vary for Kindle Fire owners, but what I have tried to address are some of the more common ones that are reported by individuals that own the tablet.

I hope you found the solutions that I have suggested helpful.

Conclusion

Thank you for reading *"New Kindle Fire HD Manual: The Complete User Guide to Master Your Kindle Fire HD 8 & 10 (Newbie to Expert)."*

This book was designed to help you master your Kindle Fire HD 8 & 10 device and get the most out of all the features Amazon has added to it. From accessing Amazon's vast Kindle library, including free book features, to purchasing and renting new movies, capturing special moments, and even troubleshooting potential problems you may face, I hope that you were able to learn a great deal about how you can get the most out of your device.

If you enjoyed this guide, please take the time to review it on Amazon Kindle. Your honest feedback would be greatly appreciated!

Thank you!

Check Out Other Books

Please go here to check out other books that might interest you:

How Do I Set Up My Kindle Fire HD: A Complete Guide for Setting Up Your Kindle Fire HD Device by Alex DaSilva

Amazon Kindle Fire HD 10 Tablet Manual: The
Complete Kindle Fire HD 10 User Guide
(Troubleshooting, Tips and Tricks Included)
by Wesley Collins

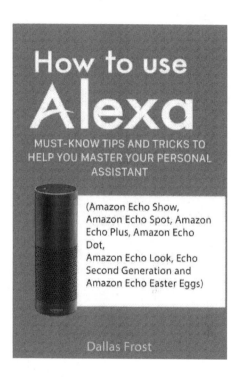

How to Use Alexa
by Dallas Frost

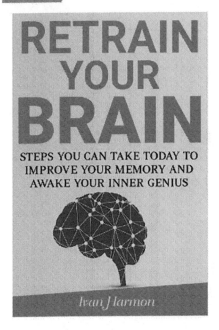

Retrain Your Brain: Steps You Can Take Today to Improve Your Memory and Awake Your Inner Genius by Ivan Harmon

Boost Your Brain Power: Learn Better, Smarter, and faster - Scientifically Proven Guides to Sharpen Your Focus and Retrain Your Brain

by Ivan Harmon

What Your Boss Never Wants You to Know:

How to Find Your Strengths, Work Happier,

Grow Your Expertise, and Rediscover Your Life

by Lam Thanh Hue

67183014R00068

Made in the USA
Middletown, DE
19 March 2018